More Praise for *The Pear*

The Pear Tree: elegy for a farm unequivocally establishes
Bethany Reid as one of the foremost poets of the Pacific
Northwest. The poems, vulnerable and full of tenderness,
fairly glitter with the detail and deep past of a childhood
home on Elk Creek in Lewis County, Washington State.
This book is a great gift.

—Priscilla Long, author of
Crossing Over: Poems and *Holy Magic*

THE
PEAR
TREE
*elegy for
a farm*

THE
PEAR
TREE
elegy for
a farm

Bethany Reid

MoonPath Press
Sally Albiso Award Series

Poetry
ISBN 978-1-936657-80-3

Cover art: *The Beekeeper's House*
by Michelle Bear

Author photo: Annie Reid

Book design: Tonya Namura, using Adobe Garamond Pro

MoonPath Press, an imprint of Concrete Wolf Poetry Series,
is dedicated to publishing the finest poets
living in the U.S. Pacific Northwest.

MoonPath Press
PO Box 2220
Newport, OR 97365-0163

MoonPathPress@gmail.com

http://MoonPathPress.com

for family, here and hereafter,
especially in memory of my grandmother,
Arada Taylor Lusk, 1898-1984

Contents

THE
PEAR
TREE
elegy for
a farm

Time is absurd. It flows backward.
It is married to the word.
                    —Ruth Stone

Long after Eden,
the imagination flourishes
with all its unruly weeds.
I dream of the fleeting
taste of pears.
                    —Linda Pastan

The Pear Tree in Winter

Crust of snow
brittle as childhood

memories, bread
sacks over thick socks,

your big brother's boot prints
across the white

orchard, creak
of the pear tree's

ice-burdened branches,
one pear,

clinging past its season,

dangling
just out of reach.

In the Beginning

Willapa Hills, Southwest Washington State

Everywhere, the smoke of other lives.

The farm belonged to our maternal grandparents,
then belonged to us, a quarter section
of land logged in the nineteen-aughts.

My grandpa's team of horses, his beehives
and plowed fields, his apple orchard,

my grandmother's two-acre garden,

their fifteen children. I knew the farm
growing back in trees, seedlings sprouting
in hayfields. We kids ran from fence-line

to fence-line every summer day,
our small herd of cows, our pigs and dogs

and feral cats, and something, *someone*

more, a thin membrane stretched
between our days and the ephemeral past.

Strawberries freckled meadow grass.
Above stanchions in the old milking parlor
our mother and her sisters had penciled

names of favorite cows, *Daisy, Berry.*

What did we hear in the silence
between notes of creeksong, birdsong, rain
on leaves, shadows of black-tail deer—

beaver, coyote, bear? Had Klallam
or Chehalis children once built

stone dams in our creeks?
What was it belonged
only to the land itself? What was it

we called *ours*?

The Blessing

Not all things are blest, but the
seeds of all things are blest.
                    —Muriel Rukeyser, "Elegy in Joy"

Your father bought the seeds
at Kaija's Feed & Tack,
bags as big as you of mixed alfalfa and timothy.
He poured the seeds into the hopper,
dragged the hopper across fields behind the tractor,
dropped the seeds into soil the plow
had wrenched open.

        And when summer came
and the field blossomed with thistles and tansy,
your father said nothing,
only frowned and turned away.

Even so, the table had to be set for supper.
Mother, Father, older brother, younger
brother, younger sisters, you,
all heads bowed, eyes closed, your mother's hand
on the metal tray of the highchair
to keep the baby from banging her spoon.
Your father said the blessing, blessed the food,
blessed the hands that prepared it.

        The path through the field leading to the creek,
a flock of ravens scattering at your approach,
their raucous, tuneless praise.

When She Was Invisible

In the basement
between walls
of stacked firewood,
the child closes
her eyes. No one
can see her
if she can't see.
Being invisible
makes her smaller,
strips her of words.
Being invisible is
her strength, a cloak
like heroes wear
in her brother's comic books.
She closes her eyes,
takes each sin
into her core. Hacked
into stove-lengths,
how bright
the world burns.

Trespass

We prayed, *Forgive us our trespasses
as we forgive...*

sin, only a fence
to be crawled under,
a warning wired to a gate,
the path beyond the gate calling us.
Give us this day

our daily bread, we were taught
to pray in Sunday School,
though it was our mother
baking our bread, its yeasty,
sweet smell tugging us home.

To thine be the kingdom,
we prayed, though maple, red alder,
Doug fir, cedar and spruce
were the kings of our kingdom,
the boundary corners of our woods
marked with stone cairns.

Nature was God's other book
and we memorized it,
fervent as acolytes.
We knew *the power and glory*
of running barefoot, sunburned,

our sweatshirts snagging on barbed wire
as we trespassed the years.

The First Temptation

We lived on Elk Creek, two miles
from the nearest town, Doty
with its clapboard churches, its post office
in the back of the general store,
plank floor pocked by spikes
from loggers' boots. Elk Creek Road
was packed gravel. Summers,
trucks dumped more gravel, one truck
coming behind spraying oil
to settle the dust. Weeds crept up
from ditches: horsetail, tansy ragwort,
curly dock, Queen Anne's Lace,
which we called wild carrot,
though it was poisonous, never to be tasted.
We were allowed to ride our bicycles
halfway to our cousins' house
and they could ride their bicycles halfway
to ours. We scratched our names
into the telephone pole standing there,
its reddish trunk redolent of the tree
it had been, and left little gifts,
offerings of leaves and sticks.
When the road was paved and striped,
a solid yellow line, white dashes
like a code, we felt as though our Eden
had been violated, made-up, dressed
in a harlot's clothes. Traveling that road,
how could we help but be tempted away?

After the Fall

My crime, I don't recall.
"Go cut a switch,"
my mother said, handing me
a knife from the kitchen drawer.
In the woods between house
and barn, I stripped leaves
from an alder shoot.
The blade of the knife was dull
as my mother's memory
would be as she aged.
A towhee sang.
I stripped leaves away,
carrying back
only the thin bare switch.
My memory keens still
with the feel of it against my legs.

World Book Encyclopedia

D fell apart at the color plate of dogs.
Under G, gems dazzled
with exotic names, ruby,

tourmaline, topaz. We adored
the solar system with its twirling planets,
opened H so often to Human Anatomy

our fingerprints grimed
the transparent overlays,
bones, organs, muscles, skin.

Nights, I whispered breeds
of horses like a prayer—
Arabian, Morgan, Paint,

Appaloosa, Palomino…
I was always the child most keen for study,
reading novels about India

and China, the moors
of England, the moons of Jupiter.
How did grown-ups stand

this ordinary life of house and barn
and church, same duties,
same faces, same meat and potatoes

season after season, when the world
in books beckoned? Yet there was
our mother, satisfied to call

our five names aloud: her India,
her Appaloosa, her bright moons.

A Haunted House

The house we grew up in was large, multi-
syllabic. It babbled and raved
in more than one language.
Here, where our mother had been born,
where our ancestors played out their moment
on the stage, where our lives, too,
would blossom. In the living room
green leaves twined and whispered
above scarred wainscotting.
Across the creek from the house,
logging trains dragged sparks
through dreams, clanking wheels,
screeching brakes. Our father's books
muttered on disordered shelves, old men
who had been to war. It was a house
that held onto its secrets. We found
in the attic some other child's
Lionel Train, found a fat dictionary,
pages glued together from P
to T by the steady drip of decades,
found a box of empty perfume bottles
shaped like violins. Children, we danced
to their music, inhaled their fruits
and florals, dreamed the brocade
and damask of other rooms.

Rapture

Our childhood summers were watery
like mystics say of the soul.
Green pond, creeks running to rivers,
salt wave. Smoke from chimneys
eddied and swirled. Little brown birds
waded through trees. Raptors
wafted, buoyed on currents of air,
Foxglove waved purple fingers
like sea anemones. In our Pentecostal church,
tongues and prophecies promised Christ
would come back for us,
that we'd meet him in the clouds.
In our subscription to *Life Magazine*,
refugees huddled on a raft,
half-naked children, wide eyes.
But wasn't the Rapture
a raft big enough for all of us?
Heaven would be as much ice cream
as we wanted. It would be like
love in one of those novels
our babysitter read, wrapping us
in its arms, "rapturous."
Heaven can break out anywhere,
so Jesus says in the parables,
like on our farm where spring water
bubbled up unexpected in the middle
of a field, crystal clear and cold.

Tribulation

We were raised on Revelations, the preacher
every Sunday morning promising hell-fire

and damnation. When the four horsemen
of the Apocalypse came riding into our barnyard

they'd seem ordinary as our rowdy uncles
jamming on Grandma's upright piano,

and the Whore of Babylon, only our great aunt,
her hugs made of cigarettes and beer.

Our bachelor neighbor chased us kids away,
shouting *Trib-u-lay-shun!*

but with such glee his syllables jangled,
silver coins in the church collection plate,

bright chords in our uncles' honky-tonk songs.

The Cow Who Dreamed of the Moon

Your uncle's black cow is the cow
that jumped over the moon. Ask Mother Goose,
ask Chagall. Though she lands on the other side
of fence after fence, fences
were never her aim. On the scrubby hillside
above the barn, your uncle's gamecocks
strut, feathers of magenta,
turquoise, cerise, halcyon blue—
cocks strolling, cockadoodling as they stretch
razored talons. Cockfighting breeds
a bird to a love so pure it will kill to have it.
The cow's udder hangs pendulous,
plump as a balloon, an udder so moonlike
itself the cow can't help leaping
over her own reflection
on the creek's satin surface. She's a cow
to bring in the next millennium,
a moon-faced calf every winter for a thousand years.
Preposterous cocks, shaggy dreaming cow,
hill farm set like an Ibsen play—
or make that Chekhov, his moon, his bridge
of stars, tall fir with a cloud like a tendon in its beak.
Goddamn, your uncle says, wiping his eyes,
wiping the barrel of his rifle
on his red plaid sleeve.
Goddamn, he says, *but she kept jumping that fence.*

To Carry On

My grandmother's name was Arada—
in another language, "fertile field."
I am the second child of her eleventh
and grew up next door

on the old creek road. When Grandma
was old, she took six pills a day,
thought she saw babies
on the chair, on the pillow, on the floor

beside her bed. "Careful," she said,
"don't sit on the baby."
Her daughters cared by turns,
moons orbiting a planet.

From the threshold once
I heard her call, "Don't forget me,"
but I had already turned
into the hall, to a time before

names were spoken.
My aunts clucked their tongues
and counted pills. "She's never
been sick except to have babies."

They smoothed a blue blanket
under her chin, smoothed back
her black hair. When I dream
my grandmother, my dream

is a word from a wordless deep,
a shaft of light. She is tiny
and wrinkled. I wrap her in my arms.
I bear her up the stair.

Such Good Work

And there appeared a great wonder in heaven;
a woman clothed with the sun, and the moon
under her feet...
                    —Revelations 12:1

She slips back along the creek
dark eyes glittering, back like she promised,
for Christ's thousand years of peace.
She doesn't knock at the door of her house
now twice other-owned.
She inherits the earth.
Where's the gray dinette with its matched vinyl chairs,
the Siamese tom stalking plastic flamingoes,
their rosy noses flush
in the woman-faced pansies,
Calla lilies opening white mouths?
She puts beans in a kettle to soak, rummages
the humming Frigidaire for a tail-end of ham.
The farm pulls itself together,
quivering off new construction. Fir trees
wait to be clearcut. Cows scatter
and the red barn rights itself
like the drybones vision of Ezekiel, *a noise,*
and behold a shaking, and the bones came together, bone
to his bone. Even in the Millennium
chickens have to be fed, necks wrung,
garden seeds poked into soil, long beans reaped.
Calluses whiten her palms. Shelves fill
with canning jars, stars in her crown.
The creek road narrows and curves.
Fifteen kiddies slam the doors.
Baby's wrinkled face presses
against her milky breast. She bakes bread,
slathers the butter on. Come Saturday night

she'll sweep and scrub. *Praise God for the work,*
she'll say, serving Christ another bowl
of cobbler, steaming berries cradled in cream.
She'll put her feet up, lean forward
to rub a sore toe, a faint smell
of perspiration and lilac powder rising
from her paisley housedress, pale
in the kitchen light as a white robe, his name
in Armageddon's ink across her forehead.
Lord, she'll say, *Lord, such good work.*

Inventory of a Matriarch

You have no baby photo of her.

A tortoiseshell comb, provenance unknown.

A photograph of her father, who slapped her for whistling.

The tune she whistled, "Shoo Fly, Don't Bother Me."

A photograph of her parents, shortly before
her mother was "killed by a train."

The blue ribbon with which she tied the end
of her braid each morning before tucking it into a bun
at the nape of her neck.

A wooden spoon for stirring a pot of beans,
for spanking a willful child.

The wooden bowl where bread dough
rested under a damp towel.

A butter churn, glass with a red top, a wide wooden paddle.

Number of rooms in her house: 18.

Number of children, including the baby who died,
whose posthumous photo hung in the hallway: 15.

These, the iron laws by which she reared her children.

From her King James bible, these verses known by heart.

Her favorite hymn: "When the Roll Is Called Up Yonder."

The stars that guided her: your same stars.

The Kingdom of Childhood

Childhood is the kingdom where nobody dies.
—Edna St. Vincent Millay

Hereford cow and calf.
Tall brown grass
clicking with insects. Jab
of barbs on a wire fence.
Creek rushing away. Patch
of blue sky over an ungrazed
field. Unglazed bowl
blue. A rustic painting, acrylic
on board. Barn staggering
under its gambrel roof.
Gamboling calves. Boards
sinking, stink of barnyard muck,
black boots with their one
red stripe stuck in that memory.
Staccato bark of the farm-dog.
Crescendo of birdcall.
Gnarled apple trees draped
in moss. Honey bees on yellow
and blue plumstains on the path.
Common pear tree, *Pyrus communis.*
Well water, dark, deep, a child's
reflected face. Grass knotted
with bullthistle, bumblebees
burrowing into purple crowns.

To Bless

My grandmother's pear tree shaded the path
that led to the beeboxes. In late spring, a frenzy
of blossoms, white like a wedding.
In late summer, our barefoot dance,
bees baptized in fallen bodies of pears.
"To bless" comes from Old English *bledsian*,
from Northumbrian, *bloedsian*, druids
in moonlight, stones hallowed in blood.
The vestibule beyond our church's front doors
had walls painted yellow as pollen, yellow
as our honey, tasting of blossoms. In church,
one blessing, hum of hymns washed in the blood
of the lamb. On the path to the bees, this blessing,
the pear tree, limbs raised, bursting with bees.

Out of the Furnace

We weren't Catholic, though looking back
I see him as a sort of priest—
my redheaded older brother, tasked
like some antique authority
to know every twisted place, every disjointed
thing or how to disjoint it.
When he picked up a Daddy-Longlegs,
it pointed to the field where we'd find the cows.
Red and black ants scooped into
his rusty Red Flyer wagon
battled to the death. He'd sic our dog
on any other dog that sidled past the gate,
and cats landed always on their feet,
no matter how many times he tossed them
to the shed roof. In the trough
where we cooled milk cans for the dairy,
he baptized kittens in the name of Father, Son,
and Holy Ghost. I, his mute witness,
altar girl to his every rite. So it wasn't surprise
that shot through me when he swung wide
the furnace door, when he drew from his pocket
a garter snake and flicked it into the coals.
Did I see vestigial feet exposed
as flames licked up, or was it only
that I believed whatever my big brother
told me to believe? It was biblical, he said,
proving Genesis: if God cursed
the serpent to crawl on its belly,
then it must have once had feet.
He told me that God had placed "enmity"
between the snake and all of womankind,
though I felt only pity for it,
the garter snake, burning,
that had never told me anything but truth.

Maeve

In the back of my mother's closet
I found a Fuller's Grocery bag
spilling with an abundance of yarn.
A baby sweater, Mom said,
the yarn a pale pinkish brown
like dogwood blossoms not yet open.
Mauve, she called its color,
and I thought of the fairy queen Maeve
in my book of tales. One shoulder
was finished, most of one sleeve,
all of the panels, the bottom border
unraveling. She had begun the sweater
for me, or maybe my next-younger sister,
had meant to finish it for the baby,
now walking and talking,
too big for anything so delicate.
Put it away, Mom said,
so I tucked the bag back
in her closet where I'd found it
behind the shiny high heels
she no longer wore and a souvenir doll
in a water-stained box. *Souvenir*
means to remember. Aged eight,
I felt the weight of all that would be
forgotten. The ball of yarn
inside the unfinished sweater,
an egg in an abandoned nest.

The Wreck

It was winter, blackberry vines
dying back, when my older brother spied
the battered pickup truck
on the steep hillside below the barn.
That summer we wore a trail
crawling through brambles to the wreck,
thorns biting our knees and arms.
Lichen scrolled across the paint,
and rust had long ago locked shut
the doors. The upholstery was worn to springs
like a corpse to bone. We tugged
the steering wheel and choke,
tried to loosen the gas pedal
from the grip of time. I wanted to ask
Mom and Dad how it had come to be there,
what uncle or older cousin had driven it
over the lip of the hill and walked away.
My brother said it was our secret
and not to tell. And then, he gave it up,
leaving the wreck behind without a shrug
or a backward glance, easy in his choices
as he would be a few years later, giving up
his childhood faith. One more time I went alone,
sole survivor of a disaster I still can't name.
Windshield a sky of cracked glass,
October berries sere,
bramble leaves dry as parchment.

Faith and Doubt

In our King James Bible, *faith*
as a grain of mustard seed

could move mountains. The mustard seed
was small. At the bible

bookstore, you could buy one
set in Plexiglas

and silver, a charm to dangle
from a chain. My faith

was at least as big
as that, and maybe bigger, the size

of the pocket watch
my father carried, its cover

opening with a soft click,
its *tick tick*. I had faith

my faith would swell larger
as I grew, like my heart,

which I learned in fifth-grade Science
was the size of my two closed fists

and beat one hundred thousand
times a day. Then doubt

crept in. Like a wasp
encased in a gall,

how it prickled to get out.

A Pee Chee of Lined Paper

Her brother is old enough this fall
to stay after school for sports.
She walks the hill-path to the barn
wearing his boots, a Pee Chee
filled with lined paper
tucked under her sweatshirt.
She is a new creature, his chores, now hers.
Slop the pigs, toss hay from the hayloft
for the cows, count the cows,
go out into the fields to search
if any is missing. Last year, tagging along,
she piled feed sacks on a rail
of the calf pens and called it
a horse, a length of braided twine,
a bridle. This year she hides pencils
and paper in a nook under the eaves.
The cows and half-grown calves
trudge in, bumping and nudging
to the mangers. At the house, her mother
scolds: "Your brother would be there twice
and back, the time you take."
She slips back into her old skin,
freckled, small. Piano to be practiced.
Table waiting to be cleared of folded laundry
and set for supper. Little sister,
crying to be picked up.

Manna

The gate wore a patina of age even then, cedar posts
faded gray, its latch made of a big nail

and a wire hoop rusted fast. Winter swooped in
with wind and sleet, cumulonimbus clouds

stacked over the low hills like batting in an attic,
locking away all thoughts of spring,

as if never again blossoms and new leaves,
never again summer with its bare legs

and skinned knees. No matter
the weather, there were cows to feed,

bunching at the gate until someone
climbed the hill path to the barn, cows

trailing behind like the Children
of Israel following Moses

and the pillar of fire. Thrown down
from the barn loft, hay tasted sweet as manna.

Each day I try to lock the past behind me,
but like manna in the wilderness, one day's work

can't be carried over to another. Each day
here stands another memory, hungry,

murmuring. *Such labor was sweet*
I started to write. But weren't my fingers

reddened by cold? Didn't the handed-down
barn boots pinch and blister my feet?

All Things Done in the Body

When, as a child, I heard the verse from Corinthians
about the reckoning after death
of "all things done in the body,"
I thought of the house
my aunt and uncle bought for salvage
the year they first married. I was ten
or eleven. Marriage looked to me
like a kind of afterlife, a new name, a white dress,
a laying aside of childhood's chores
for a brighter prize. They didn't buy the property,
only the building itself, whatever could be
dismantled and hauled away, moldings,
floor boards, windows, joists and beams,
cabinets, light fixtures, patio bricks,
cinder blocks. There must have been much
that couldn't be saved, rotted
or termite-ridden, ripped carpets,
worn Formica, glass so pocked
it had to be tossed, breaking
with a crescendo on the slag heap.
My aunt was young. She wanted a baby.
I picture her on a spring evening
weighing in her hands a fragment
for scrap or reuse, listening to the throaty song
of frogs, the whirr of bats, the screech
as her husband pulled another nail
from a two-by-four, then hammered
the bend from it before tossing it
into a bucket of nails. My aunt,
leaning in a doorway half-broken apart
must have seen the future stepping toward her
or tugging her like a thread
into the labyrinth of her life.
All things done in the body.

Like the cherry tree in the front yard
of that ruined house, she, too,
shivered beneath a mantle
of blossoms.

Failure to Thrive

As a little girl, I pretended
I was a horse. Not just a game,
but a fever for whinny

and stomp. Later, I pretended
I had a horse, barn twine bridle,
a switch of alder, slap of my heels

his hooves on the path.
I read horse books by Walter Farley
and Marguerite Henry. I read my copy

of *The Lost Pony* until the binding fell apart.
Years of this, pretending
and pretending, before my parents

gave in and let me have horses,
a bay gelding called Rebel,
a sorrel mare, Brandy. Brandy was not

a good riding horse, but we had her bred
and while waiting for her foal,
I pretended a whole future of horses,

a horse-y husband, a stable
with red and white doors,
seven or eight horse-crazy kids.

So how did all this pretending end?
With the foal, a filly, a little girl horse
that failed to thrive. I stood up

from her loss, stood alone
in the morning field, mist rising around us,
and, oh, how fierce I was, pretending

I would no more pretend.

Kairos

Not time as kept by clocks
or predicated on a sum like story problems
in your arithmetic book,
but time measured by dwindling summer creeks,
by horsetail and Queen Anne's lace
thick in the shaded ditches of unpaved roads.
There is time in that time still
for the canvas hammock strung
between cherry trees, for rainwater's scent
of rot and cherry bark, smoke
in your eyes, your mongrel dog
whining at the door, the rescued squirrel
in the hamster cage on the back porch,
speckled foal in your uncle's paddock...
But here is where time breaks apart,
seasons and years multiplied like X
in your school equations, in *current events*
where presidents are shot, where soldiers
escort children past barricades,
women in pincurls like your mother's
twisting their mouths around hate,
a man walking on the moon.
Here time divides into halves,
fourths, sixteenths, not time but Time
ticking and ticking, eyes staring up at you
from shards of a shattered mirror.

Years before Her Death

—for Lori

We rode our horses through fields bright
with dust and Canadian thistle to the creek.
At the back of the farm, ancient alders and fir trees
stood like caryatids holding up the sky.
The horses waded to their bellies,
plunging their noses where the pull of the creek
was greatest. I looped my stirrups
over the saddle horn to keep them dry.
My cousin unfastened her hair,
cupped a hand to the dark, mirroring water,
lifted it to her lips. This is the dream
of my childhood. All night I rein
my bay horse back to that still place. All night
I watch her reflection waver and beckon.

Genesis

Our younger brother once took apart
five bicycles and reassembled them as one.
Wobbling saddle, sprocket
and gears misaligned, mismatched
wheels, *flap, flap*
of a pedal, loose fender
a cacophonous screech. A puzzle
of a bike, leftover parts strewn
across the floor of Dad's shop
like bones and entrails.
I could be remembering it wrong.
Maybe it was four bicycles, or three.
My point is, in another family
this story would preface
a brother's brilliant career as an engineer,
or the best damned mechanic
in Lewis County. Oh, yes, people
would say, even as a boy
he had a hunger to know what makes things tick.
Instead, Matt is thirty years dead,
and our family, pulled apart,
is still put together all wrong.

A Green Eye

—for my sisters

On the cusp between winter and spring,
weird neon of skunk cabbage holds candles

in cupped hands. We are water skippers
crossing the old face of childhood,

landscape where moss knows no direction,
will not point us north or south.

Our children dance, bright faces
silvery fish, shafts of light amid dark pillars

of trees, air electric with birdsong.
The pond blinks a green eye.

We take turns carrying the baby.
She flaps her arms, rowing us into the light.

All the Birds of the Air

after my father retired from the woods

after his youngest son died in a car wreck

after he had the back of the farm logged off

after the quadruple bypass

after the small stroke

that he appeared to completely come back from

after that

he stopped putting birdseed in the feeder in the pear tree

yet still the birds came, house sparrow, crow,
nuthatch, brown creeper, junco,
flicker, grosbeak, mountain bluebird, towhee

and one bird, hidden in a cloak of white blossoms—

its call like a rusted hinge on a gate

after that

The Years, Cut Down

Our second-growth timber has been logged,
ground scarred with ragged stumps, brush
stacked and burned. Seedlings of Doug fir
poke green heads through grass and my logger father
says, "This one will make it," says, "not
this one," its top nibbled away by deer. He tugs it
from the ground like a weed. The year
he moved here, the year of my birth,
the timber company poisoned the deer
and for a decade all that fed on their carcasses
disappeared—coyote, turkey vulture, bear,
red-tailed hawk, bald eagle. Dad steps onto
a wide, flat stump and I climb up beside him,
kneeling to count the rings. Seventy-eight, his age.

Fallen

—for my father, in his 80th year

A winter storm has dropped
a big alder across the fence. The breach
lies on the northeast corner of the place
where the tractor road's so overgrown

he has to walk. He lugs the chainsaw
and oil can, axe and wedge,
though he'll set the wood aside
for better weather. This morning

his job is to clear the fence,
reset posts, re-strand barbed wire.
Over breakfast his wife asked what it is
on the neighbor's property that the cows

will go to so much trouble.
What does he know, but if a fence is down,
the cows are out. "It's the nature
of the beast." It's a long walk,

carrying the saw. His heart thuds
against the locked chamber of his chest
as though it, too, has a nature
to break bounds. Trees stoop

between him and heaven.
Out of the downed alder,
a jay startles, a streak of blue,
a shard of fallen sky.

Cutting Wood

Chop your wood and it will heat you twice.
　　　　　　　—old saying

My father used to say, "A woodfire
heats you many times."
He meant not only the fire,
but felling the tree,
cutting logs into rounds, hauling
the wood home to be split and stacked.
As a girl, I was never good
at chopping wood into furnace-sized chunks,
could barely lift the big axe. My father
aimed dead center, splitting apart
even a knotted log with one blow.
We had wild cherry from a storm-
downed tree. Apple wood smelled of rain.
Cedar made the best kindling.
Fir was pitchy and spat fire.
In winter, we kids packed seasoned wood
into the house, dropped it
beside the fireplace, the logs
our *Lares* and *Penates* of the hearth.
Whenever I lack the lightning bolt
of inspiration, I recall my father,
breath steaming in crisp air,
shirt soaked with sweat
over knotted muscles, heft and arc
of his axe, swift stroke to heartwood.

Because Blossoms

Because late blossoms on the pear tree   quiver
in the breeze   like hundreds of white moths
because coffee in a chipped blue mug
because the morning newspaper won't arrive
until tomorrow's mail   because insistent *physt, physt*
of the sprinkler on the garden all night   outside
your bedroom window   because all walls
are temporary and all roofs   because
the white blouse your mother   left
on the clothesline   flaps languid in a breeze
lost soul, old sister   because bluebells grow
in the tall grass   because the scent of pear blossoms
because on the back porch your father   sets aside
his crossword puzzle and dozes   because last night
constellations reeled   and an orange moon
thin as a moth's wing   fluttered over dark hills
because your life   keeps falling back on its beginning

Catastrophe—

from *kata*, meaning down,
and *strophe*, turn,

both from the Greek, a stroke
though not of luck,

dropped stitch, dropped
plate, broken step,

clock face cracked, time
stopped, barn roof

caving under the torrent,
the car, swerving

over the center stripe,
iridescence of shattered glass—

the seep and reek of it,
its shocked blooming into light.

The Fires

"Here," the doctor said, tapping the computer screen.
"A brain bleed, a toxic Jell-O."
His note on my father's hospital chart:
"hemorrhagic stroke."
This, in August, while forest fires raged
across the West, smoke hanging in the air.
The doctor was young and impatient.
He recommended surgery
to relieve the pressure. My mother
wanted to say yes. I said no.
It wouldn't undo what damage had been done.
She, too, was ill. At shift changes,
the nurses whispered to one another,
"The mother has dementia."
My childhood tilted toward the pit.
Mom used to make a salad with lemon Jell-O
and grated carrots, chunks of pineapple.
Sunshine Salad, we called it,
a miracle of suspension, like dreams one has of flight.
Summers of my early childhood, my father
fought forest fires, returning to us
smelling of a thick, nose-crinkling smoke.
We knew smoke, children of woodstove and furnace,
brushfires, bonfires down by the river.
The smell he carried home from fire-fighting
was more acrid, scorched forests,
the whinny of terror.
He propped his feet on the torn hassock
and opened the newspaper or turned on the TV news,
his choice of two snowy channels.
He fell asleep while Mom got dinner on the table.
The computer monitor in the ICU
where my father died was black and white.
Leaving the hospital that evening

after talking with the doctor, I breathed smoke
and watched the sun go down.
A bright ball of red in an orange and purple sky.

The Tree

This root [deru] gives us trust, truth, truce, tryst,
betrothal and tree.
                    —Tom Jay

What the tree knows is cambium,
phloem, pith. It plays the harp

of its heartwood, sucks down the sap-
wood, dreams of the pileated

woodpecker, its flag of red, its
staccato drumming, steady

as earth's pulse. Houses dream of trees,
the beam along the rooftop

with its straight grain, its odd knot.
The fiddle, too, dreams, whittled down

to a pure passion, what the wind
once sang in its branches.

Our Keeper of Knots, Undone

A knot is like an egg; it is either good, or it is rotten.
—Clifford W. Ashley,
Ashley's Book of Knots

Loops of bowline and crowfoot,
sheepshank and lanyard,
what scaffolds, bridles, braids us

together—parceling, worming, marling—
bight stretched tight,
scuttlebutt lashing. Fingers

gnarled, cable fixed, hooked, trussed.
We're stirrupped and coaxed, bound,
jammed. Joints unjoined, nooses, unstrung,

mouth a chained sinnet of curses.

Who holds fast or knows
how to rove through the rigging?
Ancient, artful, herringbone stitch,

hitched, fetched, hands
twined, twice-laid, matted, mated,
kinks kinked, rigging untrimmed.

The keeper frets and galls, chafes.
Whatever tethered us, holds, hobbles.
We are haltered and hammocked,

hauled, chafed, raveled, foxed,
shrouded, no cleat left us,
not a chinkle.

My Father, Growing Wings

The dreams began in August
as he lay on a white-sheeted bed in the ICU.

All through a wet autumn they continued,
the roots of my father's wings

struggling, digging their way
out of muddy earth. So much work

to support so much beauty, like men starved
and beaten to build a cathedral.

Now it is winter and my father's wings
wrap sinew and tendon deep

in my tenebrous heart. Waking,
I would have my father back, wingless.

I would keep him grounded, not lifted
by any grace save that of my own wishing,

no halo, no harp. His cracked bucket
of a voice still unable to carry a tune.

Selling the Wetlands

1.

That long moment between dusk and dark,
heavy with frogsong.

Barking of a dog on a neighboring property
and our dog's answer,
lonesome and company at the same time,
like stars clicking on above us.

After supper, homework spread across the table,
geometry and history, a map of states.
Dishes in soapy water in the sink,
potato peelings and sour milk in a pail for the pigs.

Vietnam on the television,
men trudging through mud and gunfire.

2.

We plant the "for sale" sign beside the road

and walk through bright spring rain
behind the surveyor into the fields.
"Here is where the boundary will lie," he says,
cutting apart six acres around the house
while the rest goes to a timber company.

Our boots sink into bog
yellow with buttercups and spikes of skunk cabbage.
When my sister says, "This wet land is good for nothing,"

the surveyor stops walking.
"When you file with the county,"

he says, his face grave,
"don't say *wetlands*."

3.

My heart is a geography of loss,
a pond where my too-big boots

disturbed the shimmering glop
of polliwogs, a meadow of pearly-everlasting,

twittering of nuthatches, rising call
of a Swainson's thrush,

the creek's complaint, *chirrup*
of frogs. I have folded my childhood

and laid it in a box,
but can't help tugging it out,

dusty and moth-eaten,
so tattered it keeps no one warm.

A Coil of Barbed Wire

All his life, my father taught us to choose
what matters and put a fence around it.
He unspooled a rod of barbed wire,
four-pronged, silver and sharp,

strung it along a row of cedar posts,
wrapped the ends, tightened
the length with claw-hammer
and come-along, tacked it into place.

One day he coiled and propped a remnant
of barbed wire against a stump, meant to toss
the coil into the back of his pickup truck
but forgot. He wasn't the sort

of man to leave anything unused, drank
yesterday's cold coffee so not to waste it.
The summer after my father's death
I find the hoop of rusted wire waiting in a patch

of sun, wreathed by green weeds
and small pink flowers. His cows
slaughtered or sold, my father's fences drift
like the universe toward entropy.

Lessons in Beekeeping

Upstairs in the old house,
thousands of books
wait to be sorted into boxes,
my father's scrawled signature
on every flyleaf. Louis L'Amour,
Frank Yerby, Pearl S. Buck.
Rough plywood and two-by-fours,
paperbacks in a double row,
hardback bookclub editions,
rows of Reader's Digest
Condensed Books. Elizabeth Goudge's
A Book of Comfort.
The bookshelves are a hive
of words, cacophonous barn,
dead flies on the ledges,
grizzled cherry tree tapping
against warped window panes.
My head aches with the smell
of mold and dust,
with pent-up stories. *How to Win
Souls. The Book of Knots.
Lessons in Beekeeping* inscribed
to my father's father,
"To Gene, 1918."
So many books, rhyme
without reason, rough meter
like a song long unsung.
I work through the September afternoon,
robbing the shelves,
black bear at a bee tree,
my father in a bee veil
prying up lids of beeboxes.

What's Carried Away

—for Katie

We sort through boxes of photographs
all afternoon, dog-eared, brittle

for having been left so long untouched.
My nephew's new wife is reading a novel

about vampires, and the faded images of cousins
and classmates seem no less strange. We toss

into the trash weddings we didn't attend,
shadowed faces grinning beneath mortarboards,

toothless babies whose names we can't guess.
We breathe the dust of a grandfather's first love,

of horses on parade, my niece prattling
cheerfully about her vampire-hunter

with his mirror and stake. Someone finds
a camera with film and our children

who are no longer children snap more pictures.
The pear tree my grandmother planted

a century ago has dropped its scabbed pears
in the grass. Who will gather

what we leave behind? My niece, helping
in the kitchen, tells me how her novel

sorts the living from the dead. The dishes
are only for everyday, but when they are clean

and dry, we swaddle them in newsprint
as if they are precious before packing them

into boxes to be carried away.

The Knot

A length of rope, stiff
with decades of disuse, darkened first
by much handling, the sweat
and dirt of hands

           that pushed one end
through a loop and made a loop and tucked
another end, knotting tight some task
long dropped off.

Some Glad Morning

My mother had fallen in the night.
One of her sisters called me and I drove down,
took her to the clinic to get checked out,
and then to Doty, to the cemetery, to see Dad.
It was May, almost Memorial Day
and we brought flowers. She stood over his grave
and said, "God can do anything.
He can turn back the time
and my husband will still be alive."
Was it that visit, or an earlier one
when she looked at me, eyes wide,
and didn't know who I was?
After the cemetery we stopped at my cousin's house.
Joan had just taken a strawberry-rhubarb pie
from the oven. She put on coffee.
Gospel played on the radio.
Some glad morning, I'll fly away.
If I could turn back time, that's one of the moments
I'd go back to. Everything homely
in the best sense of the word, the pie crust
perfectly golden, buttery and crisp,
local strawberries, rhubarb from Joan's garden,
the filling hot, tart and sugary,
fresh cream poured over the top.
Someone once said, *poetry is truth set to music,*
and so is pie. Truth was, the three of us,
sitting together for the last time
in a kitchen with rooster prints on the wall.
My mother, eating pie and laughing,
still herself.

The Last Time I Heard Her Play the Piano

my mother lifted her hands to the keys and it was
as if her dementia had been called out of the room
by something more urgent, the way her memory
had begun slipping from her years earlier,
a companion stepping aside on the trail
while she walked on. She lifted her hands
to the keys and played an old hymn, played
by heart, as people say. Like cupping water and
lifting it, dripping and glittering to your mouth—
that was how the music felt, and fell, filling the room,
settling weightless and bright, a goldfinch
lighting on a thistle, my mother, playing the piano,
forgetting her forgetting.

The Lost Brother

—for Matthew

Now that our mother has forgotten your name,
I see you everywhere.
In a movie, you're the spy, swapping
one briefcase for another.
You get off buses just as I find my seat,
or I catch a glimpse of you, disappearing in a crowd.
Once I saw you at a Fourth of July fireworks,
another time, late one night
in Galway. When I wear the blue sweater
I bought there, I think of you. I've never mourned
you the way I've mourned others,
and maybe that's why. I was glad
you'd escaped your busted marriage,
left behind your bad choices
like a trail of crumbs to be eaten by birds.
I've dreamed you living in a cabin
in the trees at the back of our old place,
reading Dostoevsky and writing poems.
I'm not cracked, I know you're on that hillside
where we left you, your coffin turned away
from the marker because our mother
didn't want your head down and feet up
for all eternity. Even that secret
has a way of animating you,
as if you might sit up, dust off your hands
with a *that's that,*
and step back into your life.
Our common ground was always a raft
of ice. With you gone, it's broken smaller.
Am I tired, after all these years,

of carrying you with me? I'm not.
You weigh nothing, a hole in my pocket.
I never forget that you're not there.

Heavy with Fruit

In a black and white photograph, my grandmother
stands beside a sapling pear tree

draped in sunlight. In my store of memories
she bares her thin breast

for my baby sister, unbraids her hair
at day's end. Her home-baked bread,

her bread-and-butter pickles, her white-bean soup
with ham, peppermints

in the pockets of her housedress.
The backyard chopping block,

headless chickens flopping, spattering bright
coins of blood across the grass.

Her mouth an O around a hymn, bible
open on her lap. My grandmother's pear tree

grows grizzled with age, tatted
with doilies of moss, heavy with fruit

that goes unpicked. Matisse said
he didn't paint things, only *the difference*

between things. Differences between us
deepen as I age, tree bark twisting

over a length of wire.

Everything No Longer There

And perhaps it will be pleasing to have remembered
these things one day...
      —Virgil, *The Georgics*

Maps of the place where I was born bear names
of towns that were never towns, stops on the railroad
where a water-tower stood, or a homestead
so long gone you can't find a single chimney stone.
Murnen, that's one name, grave marker
for someone's stillborn dream, like Swem Creek,
when no one remembers a man named Swem.
The creeks that ran along our farm were Deer Creek,
traveling a long way down out of the Doty Hills
before disappearing into Elk Creek. Elk Creek ran
to the south fork of the Chehalis River
along railroad tracks ripped up and carried off
when I was ten. One creek farther up the logging road
was called Eight, another, Nine. You can find
the town of Dryad on a map of ghost towns
of Washington State, but once it was real,
a sawmill town named by some lover of Greek myth.
In my mother's time: company houses
for sawmill workers, a post office, taverns, a church,
a school. We kids biked to Dryad's strawberry fields,
bought penny candy at the Dryad General Store,
leaning even then under a burden of moss and brambles.
The only reason to visit Dryad now
is Sylvan Cemetery where our great-grandparents
lie under stones, time erasing their names.
"Sylvan," though the county took out all the trees.
Too much trouble to mow around.

Dream of a Dun Mare

Lock clicked open,
gate pushed back, a dun mare

so near waking's ledge,
it was as if I held

her lead rope in my hand, tugging it
so she swung her head around,

jingle of her halter,
one pale eye fixed on me.

She was ribby,
sway-backed, freckled

with healed-over saddle sores,
her belly heavy

with promise.
Smell of cracked leather,

urine-soaked straw.
I woke filled with emotion

like a bucket with water,
sorrow at her brokenness, joy,

that down the night's steep passages
I might yet ride.

The Crossing

The last calf of the last spring
of my father's life,
it stood bawling, stuck on the west side
of the pond's green circle.
Dad called me to see
and we stood on the porch
watching through cracked panes.
A bull calf, a Hereford, so fresh
on the earth, white face and red body
still tufted where its dam had licked
the afterbirth away.
The pond wasn't deep,
except with April's muck and rushes,
the bursting of buttercups,
polliwogs poised in their jelly
like fruit waiting in apple blossoms.
The calf braced itself
against all persuasion, head down,
legs splayed, its voice a steady bellow
like a bell tolling.
We were astonished at how quickly
my father crossed from this life
to the next, the years
falling behind him like finished chores.
In the ten years that my mother declined
and lingered, I often pictured Dad, waiting,
impatient, tapping the pane
as the calf that morning
gave in, splashing through the mucky divide,
trotting up the hill path
after its kind.

The Day We Buried Our Mother

a light mist fell, the damp at the graveside
just enough to make us button our coats.
Later, we unbuttoned and peeled them off,
told stories and laughed as if we'd left our grief
piled in damp mounds in another room.
When rain ruined the harvest,
summers of my childhood, my father,
hating to waste it, put it in the barn anyway,
though maybe we would lose a cow that winter
to bellyache. The day we buried our mother,
we put up our grief exactly like that,
knowing it would later have to be eaten.

Pear

Buttering my morning toast, I use her knife
with the yellow Bakelite handle,
and my grandmother is here, shuffling
across my kitchen in her paisley housedress
forty years after her death. It is November,
month of her birth in 1898. Leaves
from the big maples are the yellow
of the knife's Bakelite handle and the yellow
of the feathers of the china hen that perched
on her shelf, yellow of the linoleum floor
where I took my first steps. Yellow
like the store-bought pear on my window sill.

The Bridle

I saved my babysitting money to buy it.
The bit is what *The Horse & Pony Encyclopedia*

calls a Pelham, and my uncle Billy
called a gag, a severe bit for my tough-mouthed

mare. Skittish, wayward girl,
reddish coat, blonde mane, cat-soft nose

beneath a wide white blaze,
four white stockings, which, my uncle said,

meant she'd turn up lame. No creature
could outdo her for sheer will.

Brandy is long buried in the past,
but her bridle hangs on a hook

near my desk. If the meek
inherit the earth, the stubborn

have their own narrow stall here,
and if a field of sorrow, another of joy.

Acknowledgments

My thanks to the editors and readers of the following publications where these poems first appeared, often in earlier forms and with different titles:

Boxcar Poetry Review: "Out of the Furnace"

Braided Way: "The Blessing," "Trespass"

Calyx: A Journal of Art and Literature for Women: "To Carry On"

Cirque: A Literary Journal for the North Pacific Rim: "In the Beginning"

Clackamas Literary Review: "The Years, Cut Down"

Constellations: "The Fires"

Crab Creek Review: "Faith and Doubt"

Five Willows: "My Father, Growing Wings"

Freshwater Review: "Rapture"

Hole in the Head Review: "Maeve"

Madrona: "The First Temptation," "The Tree"

Open: Journal of Arts and Letters: "Lessons in Beekeeping"

Passager: "All Things Done in the Body," "Cutting Wood"

Pilgrimage: "What's Carried Away"

River Mouth: "Catastrophe—"

Rust & Moth: "Pear"

Sheila-Na-Gig: "The Cow Who Dreamed of the Moon," "Genesis"

The MacGuffin: "The Last Time I heard Her Play the Piano"

Windfall: A Journal of Poetry and Place: "Fallen"

You Might Need to Hear This: "The Lost Brother"

"Years Before Her Death," "The Day We Buried our Mother," and "The Crossing" appear in the anthology, *Chrysanthemum 2020*. "Such Good Work," "To Carry On," and "A Green Eye" appear in the chapbook, *Be Careful* (Chuckanut Sandstone, 2005). A much earlier version of "To Carry On" appears in my Master's Thesis, *Calling a Daughter* (University of Washington, 1992).

"The Tree" won an Edmonds Arts Commission Poet's Perspective Prize in 2022. "The Last Time I Heard Her Play the Piano" won the 2017 Poet Hunt Contest (*The MacGuffin*). "Such Good Work" won the 2004 Jeanne Lohmann Poetry Prize (Olympia Poetry Network).

I am indebted to MoonPath Press, particularly editor Lana Hechtman Ayers and book designer Tonya Namura for bringing this book into being. Thank you to poet Sally Albiso for blazing her trail of poetry, and to John Albiso, Sally's husband, for endowing this prize in her memory.

Thank you to Michelle Bear for the gorgeous cover art.

I am thankful for my writing community, which, from the time I first blundered into Professor Nelson Bentley's evening poetry workshop thirty years ago, has embraced and supported me. My weekly poetry exchanges and Zoom meet-ups with Priscilla Long got me through Covid and were essential to the process of creating these poems and this book. Sharon Bryan, Deborah Woodard, Carla Shafer, and Francine Walls read early drafts of the manuscript and nudged me to see the possibilities differently. Special thanks to Holly J. Hughes, Karen Whalley, Madelon Bolling, Janet Blumberg, Jayne Marek, and Paul Marshall.

Thank you to all the members of the Writing Lab—Carla, Paul, Kathryn, Sheila, Janet H., Lori, Judith, Colleen,

Mike, Margaret, Thelma, and Louise. Our weekly workshops are about more than the poetry and prose we share; like a tree, they are life and life-sustaining.

Thank you to Bruce Reid and our three daughters, and thank you to my siblings and cousins for our shared childhood. Finally, I wrote these poems and worked on this manuscript always aware that my parents, Ivan Daniel King (1927-2010) and Beverly Ann (Lusk) King (1932-2018), were looking on with encouragement and love.

About the Author

Bethany Reid grew up in southwest Washington on a farm skirted by second-growth timber, in the house where her mother was born. Her father was a logger, her mother described herself as a housewife, but they were pillars of their small Pentecostal church, and the house brimmed with children, music, and books.

After earning an MFA in poetry and a PhD in American Literature from the University of Washington—her faculty advisors were Colleen McElroy and Dickinson scholar Vivian Pollak—Bethany taught writing and literature classes at the University of Washington, Seattle Pacific University, Edmonds Community College, and, for twenty years, at Everett Community College.

Her earlier poetry books are *The Coyotes and My Mom* (Bellowing Ark, 1990); *Sparrow*, which was selected by Dorianne Laux for the Kenneth and Geraldine Gell Award (Big Pencil Press, 2012); and *Body My House* (Goldfish Press, 2018). Bethany also has two chapbooks, Be Careful (Chuckanut Sandstone, 2005), and *The Thing with Feathers* (part of Triple No. 10 from Ravenna Press, 2020). Her poems have received numerous awards, including the Jeanne Lohmann Prize, and Calyx Journal's Lois Cranston Memorial Prize. Her poems, short stories, and essays appear in many on-line and print publications, including *Poetry Northwest, Adelaide, Prairie Schooner, Heartwood, Persimmon Tree, The MacGuffin, Peregrine, One Art, Catamaran, Kithe*, and *The Dewdrop*.

Now retired from full-time teaching, Bethany divides her days between walking and writing. She has a passion for writers and writing of all sorts, leads a writing group, works with writers one-on-one, and teaches poetry classes whenever she has the chance. She and her husband live in Edmonds, Washington, near their three grown daughters. You can learn more about her at http://www.bethanyareid.com.